The Quick Guide to Making a (GREAT) Living as a Freelance Copywriter

The Information You Need to Get Up and Going FAST!

By

K.M. Lashley

Copyright © 2015 Black Dog & Blue Seas Media, LLC. All rights reserved.

The content contained within this book belongs solely to the author. Sharing it, distributing it or reselling it by any means at all without express written permission from the author (ME!) is a big NO NO!

Disclaimer

All attempts have been made to verify that the information contained within this book is accurate, neither the author or the publisher assumes any responsibility for errors, omissions or different interpretations of the content.

This book is meant for entertainment and informational purposes only. You're responsible for your own success. The views contained within this book reflect the author's experiences solely and do not guarantee any other person's success. Also, just because a suggestion is presented in this book doesn't mean you have to or should take it. Use your own due diligence when it comes to making business decisions.

Also, all information, products, and services mentioned in this book are for educational and informational purposes only. Use caution and see the advice of qualified professionals. Check with your accountant, attorney, and other professional advisors before acting on these or other information, products and services. You agree that the author and publisher are not responsible for the success or failure of your business decisions relating to any information presented in this book.

Any perceived slight of any individual, organization or business is completely unintentional.

Neither the author or publisher assumes any liability whatsoever on behalf of the reader of this book and its contents. The author's and publisher's entire liability, and the purchaser's exclusive remedy, shall be a refund of the price paid or replacement of our products, at our option. We limit replacement to thirty days. All remedies are limited to the United States.

Adherence to all applicable laws and regulations, including federal, state and local, governing professional licensing, business practices, advertising and all other aspects of doing business in the U.S. or any other jurisdiction is the sole responsibility of the purchaser and/or reader of this book.

Some of the links in this book are affiliate links that the author will get a sales commission from if you use them. However, be sure to do your own research before purchasing any product online or offline to make sure it's the right solution for you.

A (Free) THANK YOU! Gift

As a THANK YOU for purchasing this book AND for taking your valuable time to read it, go to https://pageturnermission.leadpages.co/prosperouscopywritertoolkit-book1/
to get your FREE copy of The Prosperous Copywriter's Toolbox AND 3 key checklists to help you start and run a successful freelance copywriting business!

Table of Contents

Chapter		Page
Dedication		7
Forward		8
Chapter 1	**Freelance Copywriting: An Ideal Freedom-Based Business**	13
Chapter 2	**Naming Your Business**	18
Chapter 3	**The Business Side of Your Business: Who's On Your Team?**	27
Chapter 4	**Getting Real. Logos, Business Cards and Other Fun Stuff**	36

Chapter 5	**Setting Up Your Workspace: The Essentials**	45
Chapter 6	**You're Good? Prove It!: Building Your Copywriting Portfolio**	53
Chapter 7	**The Writer's Website**	63
Chapter 8	**Pricing: Where to Start**	71
Chapter 9	**Where Do Clients Come From?**	80
Chapter 10	**10 Commandments of Client Relationships**	91
Chapter 11	**The End. Yet Only the Beginning.**	95
Resources		98

Dedication

To my son, Luke, who inspires me to become the very best person I can be in every single way.

And to my Soul Sister, Deborah, who makes this journey called "life" so much more enjoyable and beautiful.

Forward

In January 2002, I took the leap and became a full-time freelance writer. Even as I think back on that time now--more than a decade later--my chest tightens and my pulse is racing. Making that move was something that pushed me COMPLETELY out of my comfort zone. I had no clients. I was in the process of adopting a precious baby boy. I had no financial cushion. I had no other source of income. I wasn't a risk taker. But I knew down to the very deepest part of my soul that this was something I *had* to do.

I'd be lying if I told you there weren't times when I questioned my sanity--particularly during that first year. I made (and still make) mistakes. Lots of them. And things haven't always worked out the way I wanted them to. But I can't even begin to tell you how glad I am that I chose the path of becoming a freelance copywriter. It's been a rewarding one in so many ways--both personally and professionally.

Since taking the leap in 2002, I've learned that I can find success as a freelance copywriter in both boom and bust economies. And I treasure the flexibility to be a much more involved parent for my young son, thrive on the creative energy generated by working with clients who understand and value what I offer, and enjoy the freedom to live life on *my* terms. Not too shabby.

A Few Assumptions

You and I don't know each other (at least not yet), but I'm going to make a few quick assumptions about you. And here they are:

1. **You like to write.** Pretty much a no-brainer. I mean, if the thought of writing makes you break out in hives, why in the heck would you be interested in starting a freelance copywriting business, right?

2. **You're pretty good at writing.** You might not be *great* at it. You might not be an Addy

award-winning copywriter or a bestselling novelist. But you can definitely string words and thoughts together in ways that others can understand. AND perhaps someone in your life (other than you mother) has said you have a real knack for writing.

3. **You're looking to live a freedom-based lifestyle, and you need a freedom-based business to help you get there. But you're not sure how all of that works.**
You might even be saying to yourself, "How can I *possibly* make any money writing? Aren't all writers basically starving—and drunk?"

Any of these sound familiar? If so, you're in the right place, my friend. I'm living proof that you can indeed make a really good living as a freelance copywriter—nutritionally fulfilled and completely sober.

Over the years, a lot of people ask me how they can get into freelance copywriting. And with very little variation, the beginning of our conversations tend to go like this:

Wannabe Freelance Copywriter #1: "I'm really tired of my job and the whole 9-to-5 grind. It's just not for me. I heard about copywriting and was like, 'WOW! I can write promotional stuff for companies and get paid for it?' It sounds so cool! I can't believe I didn't know about it. But I've been thinking that maybe I could start doing that for a living instead of what I do now, which is [SOME FIELD COMPLETELY UNRELATED TO WRITING]. I mean, I like to write. So I think I'd be good at it. But I have no idea where to start."

OR

Wannabe Freelance Copywriter #2: "I'm really tired of my job and the whole 9-to-5 grind. It's just not for me. I do a lot of writing for the job I have now, so I'm thinking I could start doing freelance copywriting for a living. But I have no idea where to start."

Me: Great, [INSERT NAME OF WANNABE FREELANCE COPYWRITER #1 or #2]! I can definitely help you get on the right path. Let's start at the beginning and talk through the process. Sound good?

Wannabe Freelance Copywriter #1 or #2: I would love it! Let's do it!

The information contained in this book includes the steps, guidance and tips I give during the early days of coaching sessions--when my students are eager to get up and going as freelance copywriters fast. The teacher in me loves to see how their eyes light up when they're learning something new and finding out how they can achieve their dreams. The copywriter in me loves the fact that there are a LOT of other people like me who love to put ideas into words that move people to understanding and to action. Helping others get their start as freelance copywriters a helluva great way to make a living.

Now, let's get started on *your* journey.

Chapter 1
Freelance Copywriting: An Ideal Freedom-Based Business

There's a lot of talk these days about creating businesses that allow people to live the life they've always dreamed of. These ventures are often called "lifestyle businesses" or "freedom-based businesses." If you spend any time on the internet at all, you'll find PLENTY of gurus pitching what they tout to be the BEST freedom-based business out there. But I don't buy the idea that there's a single best business that fits everyone. Because, for me, freedom includes enjoying what I do—not just for the money, but for the difference it makes in others' lives. For some people, that might be teaching a foreign language or repairing cars or owning a yoga studio. For me, it's copywriting.

There are a LOT of reasons I view copywriting as an ideal freedom-based business, including:

1. **You can work from ANYWHERE.**
   Literally. I've worked from the car on long trips or between meetings. I've worked in hotel rooms. I've worked on planes. I've worked from pretty much every room in my house. And, yes, as cliché as it sounds—I've even worked while sitting in a chair on the beach. (Weird, right? Who would do that on the beach?)

2. **Great content isn't just a want. It's a MUST for anyone wanting to sell something in the 21st century—including products, services, causes, and even ideas.** So as a freelance copywriter, you're providing a service that people have to have no matter what the economy is like. I've found it to be a recession-proof way of making a good living. And there's a peace of mind that comes with that.

3. **In addition to selling, content is used by businesses and other organizations to retain current customers, to build brand**

recognition and brand loyalty, to stand out from ever-growing competition, and to stay relevant in a fast-changing world. So again, these needs push copywriting to the top of the "must have" list for businesses.

4. **Opportunities to grow your copywriting business are coming faster now than ever before because technology is changing so quickly.** All of those social media posts you see from businesses? Somebody has to write them. Attended a webinar recently? It had to be written. Listened to a podcast? Again--content had to be developed for it.

5. **Operating expenses are relatively low.** There's really no need to rent office space. And equipment needs—which we'll talk about in Chapter 5, are really minimal. So you don't have to spend a lot of upfront cash (or credit) to get your copywriting business up and going.

6. **Copywriting is something you can do successfully as a side business while still**

working a full-time job. Or you can do it as a full-time career. It's really up to you how you want to structure it. (Also, before doing a side gig, be sure to check your non-compete agreement if you signed one with your employer.)

7. **Because you typically don't have to be working on-site at a client's office, freelance copywriting provides a great deal of scheduling flexibility.** As long as I meet my client's deadlines, they don't care when I do their work. And—for me—that means I can workout at the gym in the middle of the day when hardly anyone is there; I can pick up my son after school so he doesn't have to ride the bus and come home to an empty house; I can meet friends for lunch and not freak out if I stay longer than an hour. The list goes on and on. For someone who has felt trapped by corporate structure—this kind of flexibility is HEAVEN!

Now, don't get me wrong. Although I absolutely love my life as a freelance copywriter, it's not a "freedom-from-all-things-I-don't-like" business. That's not what having a "freedom-based" business is. I still work very, very hard. I get last-minute calls about changes that need to be made. I have to give up weekends and/or work through the night once in a while to meet a deadline. You get the picture. And while I make a great living, freelance copywriting isn't a get rich quick kind of scheme. So don't let anyone tell you it is. But I do have the freedom to build the life and the lifestyle I want for me—and for my family. And you can, too. Let's talk about how you can do just that.

QUICK START TAKEAWAY: Starting a freelance copywriting business can give you the freedom you've been dreaming about. But you have to put the work in.

Chapter 2
Naming Your Business

I have to say that one of the toughest types of projects clients ask me to work on involves naming--whether it's for a new product, a business, a process or anything else. There's a lot of pressure, because the right name can help set my client up for success. A not-so-right name? Not so much. And it's the same when it comes to naming your freelance copywriting business.

So, why should you start with naming your business? Because:
1. It's what you'll need when you're submitting legal paperwork for your new venture. (We'll talk about that in Chapter 3.)
2. You'll need a name when you open business accounts at the bank. (Again, in Chapter 3.)

3. It's the name you'll use to introduce yourself to potential clients.
4. It'll make you feel like you've arrived as a business owner.

If the naming process is new to you, there are several ways you can go about getting it done—including these:

Hire a naming expert. There are companies out there whose sole purpose is to come up with names. But the naming process can become EXTREMELY costly. (I know. I've seen—and sent— the invoices.) It's an option that you should be aware of. But it's not one I recommend to my coaching students who are just starting out as freelance copywriters.

Go the DIY route. Just come up with a name yourself. That's what I did. I knew I wanted the name to have something in it about communications and something about creativity. I had about a night to figure something out, so I ended up with Karacom Creative. (Kara is my first name and "com" was short for communications.) The alliteration works and it's easy for my clients to remember.

There's no magical formula for coming up with a name for a business. At least not one that I've been able to find. But there are some "Dos and Don'ts" to follow. Let's start with the "don'ts":

- **Don't get "cutsey."**—Maybe you like bunny rabbits and think the name "Bunny Rabbit Copywriting Business" would be cool. It's not. Choosing an edgy and/or creative name is fine. But remember that you want to be viewed as a professional. So your name goes a long way in making that happen.

- **Don't' make your name too long and/or too hard to spell.** This can cause all kinds of problems. If people can't remember your name because it's too long, how are they going to remember how to contact you. AND how are they going to refer you to other potential clients? Same with a complicated spelling. How is a potential client going to Google you or find you in any other way if he or she can't spell the name of your business? Remember--there are other great copywriters out there, too, who have easy-to-remember and easy-to-spell names. If you're a busy marketing manager, who are you going to call first?

- **Don't make it generic.** Okay. I'll admit that The Copywriting Business might be a fun name if the branding is done correctly. In fact, there might already be a freelancer using that name. But be careful about using such generic terms. You'd be amazed at how many copywriters try to use some form of the word "write" in their name. I get it. Makes sense. But it doesn't help them stand out from their competitors.

- **Don't use a name that's the same or very close to other businesses.** If you do, you can encounter some not-so-welcomed trademark infringement issues. When in doubt, check with an attorney.

- **Don't use the name of geographic area you're in.** Let's say you live in Smithville and you decide to call your business "Smithville Copywriting Services"--you've dug yourself a hole that can prove hard to get out of. When prospective clients see your company name--yet they live in another city (or another state or another country)--there's a pretty high chance that they're going to assume you aren't available to do business with them. Because so much of business is done virtually these days, you'll have opportunities to work with clients in many different locations. While you might *start out* locally—position your business to build a national --and even global--client roster.

Now let's look at what you *should* do when naming your business:

- **Choose a name you can also use in your website's URL.** You don't want to choose a name and then find out that someone else owns a URL (website address) that has that name in it. It happens. Believe me. Been there. Done that. Remember that some people purchase domain names and sit on them in hopes of selling them for profit down the road when someone needs a particular URL. To avoid this, check your name in a domain registration service to see if it's available before you go too far down the road. I often use GoDaddy or my hosting service, Hostgator, to do this.

- **Choose a name you current and potential customers can relate to—particularly if you're in a niche industry.** This isn't a must. But it can help set you apart from competitors, especially if you're targeting a specific industry with your freelance copywriting business. For example, if your focus is the pharmaceutical industry, consider using a pharmaceutical term in your name-- like "pharma" or "bio" or "life science."

- **Make up a word.** Google™. LEGO®. Netflix. There are a lot of quirky--yet very memorable--business names out there. And you can have one, too. But you'll need to infuse it with meaning. For instance, Google has done such a great job of doing it that we've converted the business name into a verb: "Just Google it!!."

- **It's okay to use your name for your business.** I could have named my business Michele Lashley, Copywriter or Michele Lashley Copywriting Services. I didn't. But I could have. Whether you do or don't use your name as your business name, I would STRONGLY recommend registering your name as a URL. For example, I own www.michelelashley.com. There's not a site associated with it right now. But I own it just in case.

If you find yourself having trouble coming up with a name, you might want to try the online tool called www.bustaname.com. If nothing else, you'll have fun with it!

Regardless of how you go about coming up with a name, choose something you love, that you're proud of and that says what you want it to say about your business. Get feedback from those you trust and--when possible--from those who might be in your target audience. But at the end of the day, you have to make the decision about your business name. It's one of the first decisions you'll make as a business owner--so make it count!

A Few Legal Issues

As I'll continue to say throughout this book, I'M NOT PROVIDING LEGAL ADVICE. But I will mention a few things for you to consider and--when it doubt-- discuss with an attorney:

1. As I mentioned before, be aware of trademark issues when you're choosing a name for your business. Stay away from names that are too close to those used by other businesses.

2. In some states, you might be required to register your business name with certain government entities. Where I live, I have my name registered with my county's Register of Deeds Office and with the Secretary of State. Find out what the requirements are where you live.

3. When you purchase your domain name (URL), be sure you understand all of the terms. I have my domain name on auto-renew so that I don't have to worry about forgetting to pay the annual fees and losing my right to the URL I've worked so hard to build.

QUICK START TAKEAWAY: Your business is your child. Give it a name you'll be proud of and that represents what you want it to become.

Chapter 3
The Business Side of Your Business:
Who's On Your Team?

Disclaimer: The following is NOT legal, accounting or financial advice. The information provided is solely based on my personal experiences in my own business here in the U.S. Rules, regulations and outcomes will vary from person to person. So do your due diligence!

One thing I've noticed with some folks who come to me wanting to find out how to be a freelance copywriter is that all they want to do is write. But I quickly burst their bubble, telling them that being a [successful freelance copywriter requires also being a good business person](). And that means you have to do things other than just write. Now, don't worry. These aren't things that you'll have to focus on every single day--or even every week. But--as an entrepreneur (which is what you are as a freelancer)--you need to educate yourself about them.

What follows isn't meant to be a comprehensive tome about the business side of your business. After all, this is the *Quick Start Guide to Starting a Freelance Copywriting Business.* But it is meant to give you a heads up about some of the primary issues you should be aware of.

Your Team

I don't know about you, but I don't know everything there is to know about legal matters, accounting, insurance, banking, etc. That's why I've put together a team of individuals who work in these areas and who I trust to give me good advice. So, who's on my team? Let's take a look.

Attorney

I rarely have a need for legal advice regarding my business. But when I do, I have an attorney who I go to with specific questions, such as the following:

1. Business entity formation: When I first started out, I was considered a sole proprietor for tax purposes. But as I grew, I was advised to form an LLC. So, I went to an attorney to get help with that. He also obtained my Federal Tax ID number for me. The fee was minimal and it was a pretty quick process. And it feels good to know that I'm operating under the correct business entity for both legal protection and tax purposes.

2. Fee agreements: Having a written fee agreement template helps protect both you and your clients. By hiring an attorney to draft one for you, you'll probably find that he or she will address important issues in the agreement that weren't even on your radar.

3. Intellectual property: There might be trademark or copyright issues that come up. If so, an attorney who practices in the area of intellectual property can be of help.

Accountant

I hate numbers. Really. I just *hate* them. That's why my accountant is such a key member of my team. I really can't imagine running my business without him.

For me, going to an accountant is similar to going to the doctor. It feels vulnerable and a bit uncomfortable at times. So, when I was looking for an accountant several years ago, one of my main "must haves" was that he or she be a person I could trust. (Of course, it was a given that the person had to be a really good accountant.) The one I chose was actually someone a colleague referred me to. (I always recommend asking people you trust for a referral!) He's someone who understands my business, knows what my challenges and goals are, and who is easy to have open and honest conversations with.

Even when you're just starting out with your freelance copywriting business, I think it's a great idea to go ahead and get an accountant if you don't already have one. Why? Because an accountant can help you:

1. Determine which deductions you can take to reduce your tax burden and provide guidance regarding how to document them

2. Manage bookkeeping tasks, including billing, receipt collection, and bank records
3. Determine how much to pay for quarterly estimated taxes
4. Prepare and file annual tax returns
5. Determine which business entity (i.e., sole proprietorship, LLC, etc.) works best for you at each stage of business growth
6. Provide guidance regarding business licensing and registration requirements.

I don't regret a single penny I've every spent on accounting fees. The peace of mind that comes from knowing my accounting needs are covered is priceless.

<u>Insurance Agent</u>

I know. I know. Insurance in one of the LEAST fun things in the world to talk about. But we have to talk about it.

If you work for an employer, you might have many of your insurance needs covered. But if you're planning on being self-employed, you're typically left flying solo unless you're covered under a spouse's or partner's plan. Here are a few insurance policies as a business owner:

1. **Health insurance:** I have to cover both myself and my son. So, I work with a great insurance agent who helped me find affordable options. If you're a member of a professional association or an alumni association, you might be able to access health insurance coverage through them. The Affordable Care Act has also opened up possibilities for many individuals. Do your due diligence and find a policy that works for you and your family.

2. **Life insurance:** No one likes to think about it. But, personally, I think having life insurance is a HUGE priority if you have others who are depending upon your financial support. I decided to get serious about this a few years ago because I wanted to know that my son would be taken care of financially in the event something happened to me. I contacted a life insurance agent who helped me determine exactly how much coverage I needed in order to address my son's needs.

3. **Disability:** If I get hurt or sick and can't work for a while, I want to make sure my living expenses are covered. So, I carry a disability insurance policy. It's not a tremendous amount of coverage. But it's enough to maintain my current standard of living.

There might be other insurance needs you need to explore, too, depending on your situation. For example, you might want to carry a business liability policy. Unless you're qualified to do it yourself, I'd suggest contacting insurance professionals who can help you assess your situation and determine what you need to be protected.

Banker

One of the first things you need to do when starting your business is set up a business banking account. You don't want to be using your personal account for business payments and deposits. That can cause some undesired issues.

You might want to meet with a specific banker to discuss your new business and what your plans are. I've found that to be incredibly helpful. Right now, the only business account I have at my bank is a checking account. But, you might also want:

- A merchant account that will allow you to accept credit cards. (I currently use my PayPal account for that, which works completely fine for my needs right now.)

- A business credit card for purchasing supplies, making travel arrangements, etc.

- A small business loan for any number of things. (I haven't had the need for this yet.)

A Few Reminders

Now, although I refer to the individuals above as my "team"--I don't have them on the payroll. Instead, I go to them on an as-needed basis. And--before you get all freaked out--it's really not that often and it's also not a huge expense. But it is a necessary part of running a successful business.

As you go about determining who will be on your team, keep these things in mind:

- Make sure your team members have a solid reputation in their particular field of expertise. You want people who are really, REALLY good at what they do.

34

- Choose team members who understand your business. Do they get what a freelance copywriter is? Do they have an idea about what that type of business involves? Ask them.
- Make your goals clear and bring people on board who understand them. This will make it much easier to achieve them.
- Business issues come up at unexpected times and you'll need to get answers fairly quickly. Will your team members be (reasonably) available when needed? Ask what their policy is regarding returning calls and emails.

QUICK START TAKEAWAY: Put a team of professionals together who can help you make your business as successful and worry-free as possible.

Chapter 4
Getting Real.
Logos, Business Cards and Other Fun Stuff

Now that you've decided on a name for your business, it's time to think about how you want to present your business to the world. As they say on the home improvement shows, "Let's see the big reveal!" What's interesting to me is how many writers pay little attention to this part of their business--or just skip over it altogether. Again, they just want to write. They don't want to talk about unsavory things like marketing their business. (And--yes--I'm saying that sarcastically.) This is a HUGE miss for them. But, it's not going to be for you because you're going to take the following advice to heart and run with it!

To Logo or Not to Logo

Having a name for my new freelance copywriting business back in 2002 gave me a sense of accomplishment. But when I had a logo designed for it, *that* made me feel like I had a *real* business. Here's what it looked like then:

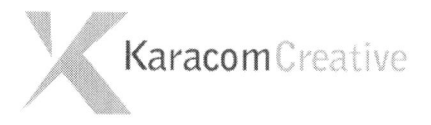

Karacom Creative

I was so proud of it! And even more than a decade later, I still like it. But a few years ago, I felt like it needed to be freshened up a bit. So I hired a former colleague who's a graphic designer to come up with something new. By that point, I knew that clients really valued my ability to create great brand stories. So the new logo (below) included a mark that turns the "K" of Karacom on its side, giving the abstract impression of an open book.

KARACOM
CREATIVE

Do you have to have a logo for your business in order to get started? Absolutely not. This is DEFINITELY not something that should hold you back from pursuing new work. But I do recommend having a logo as a way to help you stand out from other freelance copywriters in your market(s). It helps you stand out so that you don't look like just another copywriter in the proverbial pool.

How to Logo

Can you design your own logo? Yes. *Should* you? Not unless you're great at graphic design. In that case, I would advise that you don't try this at home. Step away from the computer and hire a graphic designer—one who's experienced in logo design. (Remember: Just because someone is a good designer doesn't mean they're good at *logo* design.)

Just as I did, you can go local. Maybe you know someone who can help you. Or maybe someone in your circles of friends, family and colleagues can refer you to a local designer. Because the person I hired for my logo had worked with me in the past, the process of coming up with a logo that really "fit" my business brand personality worked very well.

But what if you don't know of anyone who can help? Not a problem. You can find very talented and reasonably-priced designers through job boards like www.upwork.com and www.99designs.com.

Regardless of who you get to design your logo, be an active participant in the process. Ask to see their portfolios before hiring them and look specifically at logos they've designed. Once you've chosen someone whose work you like, help that person deliver a great logo for your business by:

- Sharing what industries you're going to be targeting

- Providing a vision of what you want your business to stand for

- Telling what you want potential clients to think of when they see your logo (For example, do you want them to think that you're a no-nonsense writer--which might be good for technical writing clients? Or do you want them to think that you're someone who's fun and comes up with unexpected solutions?)

- Showing examples of logos you like and explaining why you like them

- Providing an idea of what you do and don't want to see in your logo--like colors, fonts, etc.

- Letting them know if you want a typographical logo (like Google's) or one that has both typography and a mark (like Nike and the Nike swoosh).

What to Do with Your Logo

Once you have your logo, what do you do with it? PUT IT ON EVERYTHING! Here are a few places to consider:

- Business cards
- Invoices
- Letterhead stationery and envelopes
- Email signature
- Advertising specialty items (e.g., pens, coffee mugs, t-shirts, etc.)
- Signage (if you have an office outside of your home)

- ALL promotional materials (e.g., postcards, flyers, ads, etc.)
- Your website

Having a logo isn't a silver bullet for success. But it's a fairly small item that can make a HUGE difference in how you're perceived by potential clients. It's worth the investment of time and money because it'll help you stand apart from your competitors--even though you're the new kid on the block.

Business Cards

Although almost everything is going digital these days, people still use business cards. So I would suggest getting them to hand out when you're meeting with potential clients, during social events, etc.

What to Include

When you're designing your business card, be sure to include the following:

- Business name (and logo if you have one)
- Your name & title (e.g., copywriter, owner, brand storyteller, etc.)
- Phone number (designate mobile vs. landline)

- Fax number

- Email address

- Website URL

You might also want to include your social media info. But just for your business social media--not your personal.

Design and Printing

When I had my logo designed, I asked the designer to go ahead and set up a business card design template for me, too. Sometimes that's automatically included in a logo design package. If it is, take advantage of it. If not, this is another job you can farm out to a local designer or one you find on a job board. Also, printers sometimes offer in-house design services for business cards.

As for getting them printed, there are quite a few online printers available these days. I'm not recommending one over the other, but some you have access to include:

www.vistaprint.com

www.moo.com

www.GotPrint.com

You can also check in your local area regarding printers who are nearby. Some might give price breaks depending on how many business cards you order, so be sure to ask about that.

Letterhead/Envelopes

Should you spend the time and money getting letterhead stationery and envelopes? I'll leave that up to you. But I'll also say that I don't have either because I rarely mail anything out. Instead, I send electronic copies (PDFs) of invoices, agreements, etc.

Email Signature

Definitely include an email signature on all of your online correspondence. Not only is it professional, it also makes it easy for people get in touch with you and to share your contact information with others who might be interested.

Here's an example of mine:

KARACOM
CREATIVE

K. Michele Lashley. MA, JD
Owner
Address
Phone

QUICK START TAKEAWAY: Do what it takes to make your business stand out from competitors.

Chapter 5
Setting Up Your Workspace: The Essentials

In these days of laptop lifestyles--where people can and *do* work from anywhere and everywhere, I guess I'm still a bit old fashioned. If you're going to be a freelance copywriter--either part-time or full-time--you need a space you can call your own. One that supports efficient workflow and that inspires you to do your best work every day. It doesn't matter how big or small it is. It doesn't even matter *where* it is. You just need to have one.

So, what should go in this space? Let's focus on the following essentials:

Desk

When I first started out, I used my dining room table as a desk. And you know what? It was a pain. Although I had room to spread things out on it during the day, I had to pack it all up in the evenings. I either left it in a pile on the table hoping the cat didn't get into it or I had to take it and put it in a closet for the night. Then, the next day I had to spend time sorting everything out and getting set up all over again. Not the most productive use of time.

As a copywriter, you're going to be given a LOT of reference materials by your clients: sales sheets, white papers, articles, brochures, slide decks. The list goes on. Because of that, you need enough room to spread things out so you can see what you have. You're going to find that you're productivity increases when you have a desk with enough space to accommodate what you need.

How much you spend on a desk is up to you. But you certainly don't have to spend a lot if you don't want or if you can't right now. If you or someone you know is handy with tools, you can build one with inexpensive lumber and supplies from your local home improvement store. Places like Target and Walmart have very affordable desks. And I even got a really cool--and cheap--desk at a local flea market a few years ago. (I still have it and use it as printer table now.)

Bottom line: Get a desk.

<u>Computer</u>
Want to know where to put the bulk of your startup money? In your computer system. As a copywriter and business owner, there's nothing I depend on more than my computer.

I'm often asked if a desktop is a better choice for freelancers or if laptops work better. Honestly, it's a personal choice. Whichever type of computer makes you the most productive is the one you should get. Personally, I have both. I like the viewing comfort of a desktop. I have a 21.5" monitor that's large enough for me to have multiple documents up at one time--but isn't so large that it feels excessive. Yes--I could just use a docking station with a screen and laptop. But I just don't like that option. The only reason I have a laptop is so that I can have the flexibility to work at different locations when needed.

Now--Mac or PC? Again--it's a personal preference. I've used both. For me, Mac is the answer. But I know a lot of writers who would throw themselves in front of their PCs to protect them from oncoming traffic. (Although I don't know why their PC would be in the middle of the road in the first place.)

Regardless of whether you purchase a Mac or PC, a desktop or laptop--make your buying decision based on what you'll need long term when it comes to features like memory. It's not a good use of your money to buy a computer based only on what you need right now.

Software

I buy software based on what my clients use. And most of them use Microsoft Word, Excel, and PowerPoint. So, Microsoft Office 365 works for me. It's a monthly subscription service that ensures I have the latest versions of Microsoft Office products. I also use the free Adobe Reader to open PDFs and I have preloaded software that allows me to open zip files.

One thing I've been using more and more has been Dropbox. It allows me to upload files to the cloud and access them from any device I'm using. LOVE IT!! For now, I have the free version and that's enough. But if I need more space, I'll upgrade to a paid account.

Before investing in a lot of software--some of which you might not need--check with your clients to see what they use and let that guide the buying process for you.

Printer

I don't print everything out—but what I do print needs to be of good quality. Thankfully, you can get very effective printers for a relatively small investment. I use a Canon all-in-one printer that has printing, copying, scanning and faxing capabilities. I never use it for faxing. (I use eFax for that. See the section below.) But I use it quite a bit for the other three functions.

Fax Service

I don't use a fax machine anymore. If I need to send someone a copy of something, I'll just scan it on the printer and email it to them. But if you have a need for faxing, you might want to consider an online fax service like Efax.com. It doesn't require a dedicated fax line and is simple to use. It's what I used for several years and found it to be a fantastic solution.

Bookcase

Admittedly, a bookcase isn't a must-have item. But if you can afford one--even a small one--get one. You can use it to hold reference books, books that inspire you, and personal items that help your space feel more like your own.

File Folders and Labels

Stay organized and stay sane! And how do you do that? GET FILE FOLDERS!!

For me, using different colored folders for specific clients helps me keep track of things. One client is assigned blue, another yellow, another red, etc. As soon as a project starts, it gets its on file and label. Some people use label makers for this process. I just get the peel-off labels and write the project name on them. Quick and easy.

Don't have one file folder that holds multiple projects. That's just asking for a whole heap of confusion. Each project--no matter how small--gets its own file folder. For larger projects, it might make sense to divide things up into smaller jobs and use multiple folders.

For example, if you're working on a branding campaign, you might have one folder for naming, one for taglines, one for ad copy and one for email blasts.

Basic Office Supplies

Okay. I know this section seems like a no-brainer. But my guess is that you know the aggravation of needing to print something--only to realize the printer is out of ink. Or you've needed to mail something--but can't find a stamp anywhere, even after emptying out the junk drawer in your kitchen. A trivial as basic office supplies might seem, it's amazing how workflow can be disrupted when you're not well stocked.

Put me in an office supply store and it's like shopping for groceries when you're really, REALLY hungry. It's ridiculous, really. There's almost no office supply I can't see a need for--whether it's now or in the future. But do as I say--not as I do. The basic office supplies you'll need for your freelance writing business are these:

- Pens
- Notepads or notebooks (I tend to use a lot of Moleskine products.)
- Stapler and staples

- Sticky notes
- Paper clips
- Printer cartridges
- Printer paper
- Envelopes
- Stamps

There might be other things that you'll find you need to be efficient. But this is a good starter list. Have fun shopping!

QUICK START TAKEAWAY: Create a workspace that works for YOU!

Chapter 6

You're Good? Prove It!: Building Your Copywriting Portfolio

When it comes to getting work as a freelance copywriter, I can think of no more appropriate sentiment than "show me, don't tell me. To get higher paying projects, you're going to have to do more than just *tell* potential clients that you're a good copywriter. You're going to have to *show* them. And this is the case even if you're recommended by someone who absolutely LOVES your work. A referral will get you in the door. But, in most cases, it won't land you the job. So, what's the answer? Having a great portfolio that includes strategically selected examples of your best work.

What's a Portfolio?

When I first started working as a copywriter, a portfolio was a case (leather binders, metal boxes, etc.) in which we creative folks put hard copies of our best work, toted around to client interviews, and proudly opened as we launched into our explanation of why we were the best fit for the project at hand. Mine was so large it took up half of the backseat of my car. I spent literally hours putting my portfolio together--deciding what pieces to include, taping things into place, figuring out the order everything needed to be in. And I spent this kind of time and effort on it because I knew it was my ticket to getting to do the work I was dreaming about.

Fast forward to today and it's rare that I see any physical portfolios at all of any size or shape. Most writers, including myself, use electronic portfolios to showcase their work and also email PDFs or jpegs of work examples to interested clients. We'll talk about electronic portfolios in just a minute. But for now just know that a portfolio is simple a collection of your best work---work that you are proud to show the world, that will highlight your strengths as a copywriter and that is most likely to get you hired by potential clients.

What to Include in a Copywriting Portfolio

How Much?

One of the first questions I typically get from beginning freelance copywriters regarding their portfolios is, "How many pieces should I include?" There seems to be an assumption that more is better. But that's wrong. If you've done 20 copywriting projects but are only in love with the level of work you did on five of them--then include only those five. Period. If you include mediocre pieces in a portfolio that's supposed to represent your *best* work--what's a potential client going to think when reviewing your samples? That you're a mediocre copywriter at best-- an unpredictable one at worst.

Be sure to get permission from clients whose work you want to include in your portfolio. Remember-- unless you have another agreement with them--the work you do for your clients is theirs. Not yours.

Deciding What to Include

It can be challenging to decide what to include in your portfolio and what to leave out. To help simplify the process a bit, here are a few tips:

- Include examples of your work that represent the kind(s) of projects you want to work on. For example, if you want to get video scripting projects, include examples of scripts you've written instead of brochures you've worked on. Potential clients will want to see that have experience with the type of project they're working on. This advice also applies if you're looking to get work in specific niche. For example, if you want to work on copywriting projects in the construction industry--show projects that demonstrate your expertise in this area.

- Which projects have gotten the best response from clients? Include those--*and* testimonials from those clients regarding what they liked.

- Which projects are you proudest of? Now--it can't be *all* of them. Be honest with yourself and choose the ones you'd love to have up on a billboard for the whole world to see!

What Does a Portfolio Entry Look Like?

There's no specific format for a copywriting portfolio entry. But one format that I think works really well includes the following:

- The sample of your work--shown in its final format rather than a text document.
- A brief sentence or two that provides context for the project (i.e., what you were asked to develop)
- Details about the challenge the piece was being developed to address
- A description of the solution you provided as the copywriter
- If available, the results achieved by the final piece

The example on the next page puts it all into context:

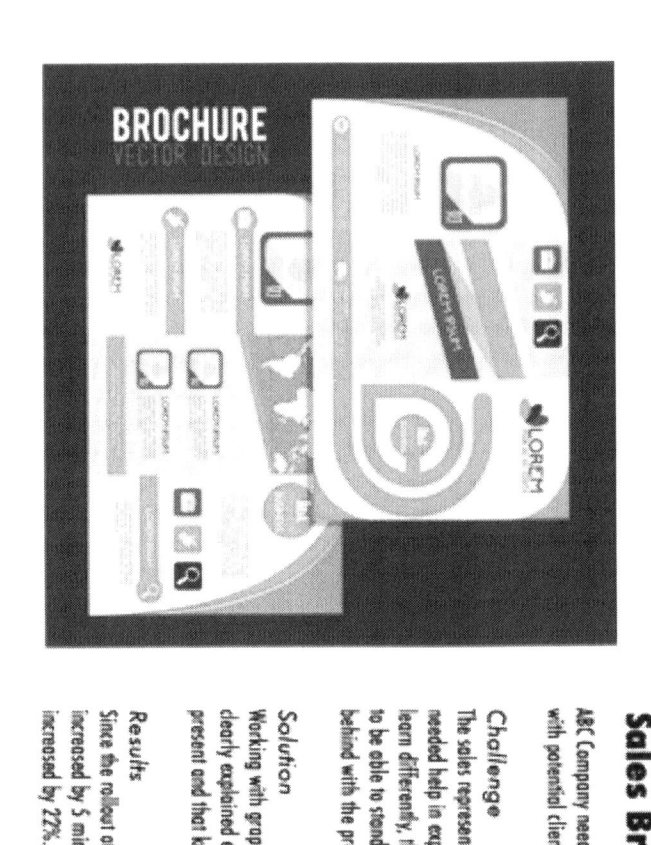

Sales Brochure

ABC Company needed a printed piece that its sales force could use in an interactive way with potential clients during sales calls.

Challenge
The sales representatives have very little time with the prospects they call on. So, they needed help in explaining various offerings in a fast and memorable way. Because people learn differently, the piece needed to be strong both verbally and visually. It also needed to be able to stand on its own once the salesperson left because the piece would be left behind with the prospect for future reference.

Solution
Working with graphic designer Joe Smith, I developed short—yet powerful—copy that clearly explained each of the offerings in a way that was easy for sales representatives to present and that kept prospects engaged.

Results
Since the rollout of the sales brochure, time sales representatives have with prospects has increased by 5 minutes and requests for proposals featuring ABC Company's services have increased by 22%.

58

Why do you need to include this information for each piece? Because you're not always going to be in the room when a potential client is looking at your portfolio. And if you're not, he or she will have no idea what role you played in creating the work, what the piece was for, etc. So you need to provide context for each portfolio entry. Also, by including this information, you're showing how you *think*. And that's more important that I can possibly say.

Getting Samples If You Don't Have Any

If you don't have any samples that show off your writing talent, don't panic. It's not uncommon for me to hear this from beginning freelance copywriters. Here's the good news: After talking with them, most find that they actually *do* have samples to pull from. And if they don't have any, they can easily get some. Here are a few ideas that should help get you started:

- **Include newsletter articles you've written** for schools, churches, service organizations, etc. (with permission, of course)
- **Include communication pieces you've done for work.** (Again--with permission.)

- **Volunteer to do *pro bono* (free) copywriting work** in order to get samples. For example, when I was first starting out, I volunteered to develop copy for a series of ads for a local arts agency in exchange for being allowed to include the final produced ad campaign in my portfolio.
- **Get creative.** Maybe you have a great idea for an ad campaign for a product you like. Consider working with a graphic designer to develop it. It's okay that it's not "real." (Of course, be clear that the work isn't "real" when sharing your portfolio with a potential client.) What you're trying to do with your portfolio is show potential clients how you think. And if that means coming up with something on your own--then that's okay. When I was first starting out, I created a full ad campaign for a watch brand that I loved. It was a relatively unknown brand, so there wasn't any advertising already out there for it. Of everything I had in that first portfolio--that made up campaign was what opened the most doors for me because it demonstrated how I thought through the creative process.

- **You can look at job boards**--like Upwork-- and bid on copywriting projects in order to get some samples. I wouldn't necessarily recommend this as a long-term approach because my experience has been that many of the jobs are very low paying.

- **You can offer various levels of copywriting services on Fiverr.com.** Again, I'm not convinced that this is a great long-term strategy. But it might help you get started with samples.

If you don't already have a portfolio of work that demonstrates your copywriting talent, make putting one together a priority. If you *do* have one, always be looking at it to see how you can make it even stronger.

Where Your Portfolio Lives

Once you've put your portfolio together, it needs a home where potential clients can visit it 24/7/365. Here are a few suggestions:
- If you have a website for your copywriting business, your portfolio needs to be housed there. We'll talk more about that in Chapter 7.

- Behance: This is a free online resource for hosting creative work. I use it and really love it. It allows me to showcase printed pieces *and* video.
- Carbonmade: This is another free online portfolio resource. I haven't used it, but I have seen that there are copywriters who have uploaded their portfolios there.

QUICK START TAKEAWAY

At the end of the day, you have to determine what will work best for you when it comes to finding a place for your online portfolio to live. Whatever you decide to do, though, make getting it done a priority! There are many times your portfolio will sell you and your capabilities faster (and even better) than you will. So spend the necessary time putting it together because it truly is one of your most powerful selling tools.

Chapter 7
The Writer's Website

I could write an entire TOME regarding how to build and promote an effective website for your copywriting business. But, for now, let's just focus on the basics. When you're deciding what information to include within your website, think about it from a potential client's perspective. For example, as a potential client, I want to:

- Be able to find all I want to know about you and your work easily and quickly

- Clearly understand why I should choose you

- Know what types of industries you've worked in

- Know what types of projects you've worked on

- Understand how do you charge (but be careful about putting fees online)

- See testimonials from previous and current clients (if available)

- See examples of your work

- Have a way to contact you

Remember, you're creating a website to be a selling tool for your business. So, be sure it answers the questions of those who are likely to hire you.

The Essential Pages

There are four primary pages you'll need for your website: home, about, portfolio and contact. Now, this doesn't mean you can't add more. But I'd advise you to focus on these four pages first and make them AMAZING! Plus, it'll help you get up and going faster if you aren't bogged down in building a website larger than you need. Now, let's take a look at what these essential pages should include:

Home

Your website's home page is the gateway between you and the work you want to do. One mistake that I see a lot of business make here (and not just copywriting businesses) is that they make the copy on their home page WAY too long. And that turns people away before they really get to see how great you are.

Use the copy on your home page to communicate what your unique selling proposition is. You want to make it clear that you are the absolute best choice for a potential client's copywriting needs--but do it succinctly.

Also, this is *your* website--so let your copywriting style shine through. Let people see how good you really are.

About

The about page is one of the most visited pieces of real estate on any website. People want to find out who they're dealing with--so they go to the about page to find out. What information should you include? Here's what I recommend:

- **Focus on your experience.** What types of businesses or industries have you worked in? What types of projects have you worked on? Do you work primarily in business-to-consumer or business-to-business?

- **Give them an idea about what your workstyle is.** Do you like to collaborate with clients? Then say so. Are you available to work onsite with a client if needed? Can you work virtually with a client who isn't local? What's your philosophy about working in the evenings and on weekends? These are things potential clients will want to know.

- **List the services you provide.** Instead of just saying "copywriting"--try to be more specific by listing services such as brand story development, new business pitches, website copy, video scripting for corporate videos, etc.

- **Mention how you charge.** Do you charge hourly fees? Or do you work on a per-project basis? (We'll talk about the difference in Chapter 8.) Mention how you charge. But I would advise against listing specific numbers.

That's information you need to provide in a one-on-one conversation.

Like your home page, the about page is a place to really let your personality shine through. There's no real right or wrong way to structure it. I tell my coaching students to just have fun with it--while also keeping in mind what a potential client might want to know about them. Want to take a look at some examples of great about pages? There are TONS of references online--but here's a good place to start: https://creativemarket.com/blog/2013/08/21/20-creative-useful-about-pages

Portfolio

Remember the portfolio we talked about in Chapter 6? Host it on your website. And remember--showcase only your best work.

Contact

You want to make it easy for potential clients to contact you. So, be sure to include your email address and phone number on every page of the site. And you also want to have a contact page. To make it easy, consider including an email form that site visitors can quickly fill out and submit.

Don't look at your contact page as just a place to house an email form and your phone number. You're a copywriter! So, make the copy here something interesting. It doesn't need to be long. But it does need to be engaging. Because by putting an effort into copy on this pages shows you're always thinking about how to stand out and be different. As with about pages, there are a lot of examples online. One place is http://www.searchenginejournal.com/25-amazing-contact-us-pages/.

Getting It Done

When it comes to building your copywriting business website, it's really never been easier than it is right now.

If you're on a shoestring budget, there are quite a few do-it-yourself options out there that make building and hosting a site simple and affordable. In the past, I've used GoDaddy and was happy with the results. Other online site builders include:

Wix

Weebly

SquareSpace

WordPress

Of course there are quite a few others, too, and I'm not recommending one over the other. Check them out on your own to see what works best for your needs.

If you have even a small budget, you might want to consider hiring someone to design your website for you. My current site was designed by a freelancer I hired through Elance and I was really pleased with both the price and the results. You can also find designers through other online resources--like 99designs--or hire someone locally.

If you do hire a designer to build your website, be sure you're really clear about:

- What you want the site to look like
- How you want the site to work for you regarding content management
- What images (if any) you want to include
- What colors you prefer
- What graphic style you want incorporated into the design

The more information and guidance you can give a designer upfront, the more likely it is you'll get to a result you like faster and easier.

QUICK START TAKEAWAYS

Through your website, you have a powerful opportunity to build your brand. It can help you:

- Stand out from the great big pool of copywriters out there who are competing for the same work you are
- Make a memorable (and effective) first impression
- Showoff your style and work
- Demonstrate how well you can sell yourself and your services (If you can do this for yourself, potential clients will have more confidence that you can do it for them.)

Chapter 8
Pricing: Where to Start

As a freelance copywriter, you'll need to determine how you're going to charge for your work. That can be a challenge--particularly if you don't really like to talk about money. And it can also be hard if you've never had to place a monetary value on the work you do. As an employee, your employer sets your salary and determines what your value is to the company. But now you get to be in charge. And that's GREAT! But where do you start?

When I began working as a freelancer back in 2002, my first real client asked me how much I was going to charge. The first mistake I made was automatically thinking I should charge an hourly fee. The second mistake I made was MAJORLY underpricing myself. I figured out my hourly fee by taking the weekly salary from my previous job and dividing it by 40--as in a 40 hour work week. The amount came to $25. So that's the fee I gave my new client. It seemed like a lot to me. But thankfully--he quickly set me straight. (I had known him for a couple of years, so he really wanted to help set me up for success.)

My client reminded me that--as a self-employed freelancer--I was now going to be responsible for paying self-employment taxes, health insurance, etc. By charging only $25/hr., I'd be lucky to have enough left over to put gas in the car. Needless to say, I bumped my hourly fee up significantly and was a *much* happier freelancer.

Now--back to you and how you're going to set yourself up for your own success from the very beginning. Here are some thoughts I have about that:

You know what I really don't like? When a client asks how many hours it'll take me to complete a project. Why? Because, more often than not, they're using that information to determine what they're willing (or able) to pay me. Their calculations are based on an hourly rate—not on what the value of the work is.

Let's look at a possible scenario: A client comes to you asking for copy for an email blast. You're a pretty fast writer. So, it might only take you an hour to finish the assignment. If your hourly rate is $70—you'd get paid $70 for your work. But, does that represent the true value of the email blast copy? What if that eblast helps your client bring in leads for thousands or tens of thousands of dollars worth of new business? That $70 pales in comparison, particularly when you realize that taxes still have to come out of that fee. It's simply paying your for your time—not your expertise or your strategic insight.

Now—let's be fair—it's not our clients' fault for asking about hours. They're just doing their job. Putting budgets together by figuring out how many hours everyone will be contributing to a project makes sense —at least for the client. It provides cost predictability and a simple (although not necessarily accurate) way to track progress. So I get why they ask freelance writers and other contractors for hours. But here's why I don't like it:

Rarely do I hear, "How many hours will you need to develop the highest quality product for

us?" Instead, it's often, "I know this is last minute, but can you get this to us by tomorrow?" In other words, they want the highest quality product created and delivered in the fewest number of hours. And because we don't want to lose the opportunity, what do many of us say? We reply, "Sure! No problem?" By doing that, we're hoping to be seen as the freelance writer who doesn't give them any problems, who is there for them for whatever they need, and who is willing to do whatever it takes. Our hope is that our willingness to do more work for less money and in less time will demonstrate our loyalty and dependability—setting us apart from other writers they could bring in. But does it do that? I don't think so. Instead, it ultimately weakens our negotiating position and continues to reinforce the VERY wrong assumption that writers offer a commodity product.

Here are the reasons why quoting an hourly fee—particularly one that's in the lower range—can be bad for your writing business:

1. **If you start with a lower hourly fee, it's going to make it difficult to ever raise your rates with that client.** When you

quote an initial hourly rate, it's understandable that a client would think that's what you believe is fair. How many times has a client every acted surprised by how low your rate is and suggested that you significantly increase it? NEVER?? Yep. That's what I thought.

2. Take another look at the example at the beginning of this post. When you consider such a scenario—which isn't an uncommon one—can you see how **it has the potential to lessen the value of what you do and what we do collectively as writing professionals**? We have to earn the respect of our clients and of the business world in general. And part of doing that is ensuring that you get paid for value—not simply for time.

3. **Charging by the hour limits your income.** There are only so many hours in the day—and, unless you're superhuman—you're not going to be doing billable work during all 24 of them. Again, taking that eblast copy job used in our earlier example, what if you were to charge a flat fee of $350 for it based on the

concept of value? Suddenly, your income potential increases significantly if you apply that to most or all of the projects that come your way.

4. **If you quote a lower hourly fee to a client, odds are you're eventually going to become frustrated with that client and the work you're doing for them.** And you're also more likely to struggle financially. There's nothing much worse that working your butt off and still feeling that very painful pinch of financial hardship at the end of the day.

So what can you do to make sure you don't fall into the trap of working by the hour? Here are a few suggestions:

1. **Charge a flat fee based on value.** There are pricing guides out there that can help you determine what a fair flat fee would be for different projects. (I'll be putting one together for Page-Turners, too. So, stay tuned.) Also, if you have a friend and/or colleague who works in the field you're writing for, consider asking

what his or her company would be willing to pay a writer for a particular project.

2. **If a client insists on working under an hourly fee arrangement, then do two things:**

    Set your hourly fee at the higher end of the fee spectrum for your level of expertise.

    AND

    Make sure you estimate the number of hours not on how fast you can write—but on how long it will take you to create a superior product.

3. If a client doesn't like your estimate (whether it's a flat or hourly fee) and has indicated they won't be able to pay you a fair price for the work you'll be expected to do—**don't take the job**. Yes—I know it can be hard to turn work down. But, what I've found is that it's typically the best choice for me and my business—not to mention my sanity!

As professional freelance writers, we want to distinguish ourselves on the value we bring— not how low we can go on our pricing. The latter is a game anyone can play. But, the former is one that requires business savvy, professional confidence, and a renewed sense of self-worth. **You're worth it! Believe in yourself and the value you bring.**

QUICK START TAKEAWAYS

- Before you start looking for clients, determine how you want to charge so that you can speak about fees confidently.
- Not sure how much to charge? Ask other freelancers in your geographical area and/or in the industries your targeting what the going rate is. You can also ask people who hire freelancers.
- REMEMBER--You don't get to keep every penny of what you make. So set your fee taking this into account. For example, taxes and operating expenses need to be paid.
- Don't be afraid to charge what you're worth. Starting out, I wouldn't go any lower than $50/hr.
- Flat fees are a good choice if you work fast and have a well-defined project.
- Hourly fees can be a better choice for projects that aren't clearly defined and/or don't have a set end date.

- Don't go low with your fees trying to underprice competitors. It's not fair to you or to our profession.
- Be open and clear about your fees when speaking with current and potential clients. If you're not comfortable talking about money-- find a way to at least be okay with it.
- Get a fee agreement in writing.
- Remember that you and your work are worth a fair fee. As copywriters, we help build brands, increase revenue, move people to act, spark change
- As you set fees, think about the value you're providing to your clients. This should make it a little easier to set fair fees.

Chapter 9
Where Do Clients Come From?

One of the questions I'm asked more than any other by new freelancers is this: "How do I get clients?"

It can be daunting. I mean, after all, when you start out, clients aren't going to be knocking on your door like they most likely will be later. Instead, you'll have go out and find them. But where do you start?

Before you start cold calling (and/or cold emailing) potential clients, put some thought into the types of clients and industries you want to work with, as well as the types of projects you want to do (e.g., website copy, ad campaigns, brochures, video scripts, etc.). Write this information down instead of trying to keep it in your head.

When you're first starting out, you might feel yourself willing to take anything and everything that comes your way. I get it. Been there. But try not to give into that feeling--at least not for long. You want to be as strategic as possible in how you build the foundation of your business--particularly when it comes to your client list.

By thinking about what types of industries you want to work in, you can target your client search more easily. For example, you might have a background in construction. So, it would make sense for you to target local builders, architects, plumbers, electricians, engineers, etc. Your experience with the work they do will help give them confidence in your ability to understand their communication and marketing needs. It doesn't mean you can't also do work for other industries. It just gives you a stronger starting point.

Once you have at least a general idea of the industries you'd like to target with your new business develop efforts, here are some potential client pools to explore:

- **Corporations** are great sources of regular and well-paying freelance writing jobs.
  Who to contact: Look for titles like marketing manger, brand manager, VP of marketing communications, etc.

- **Small business** are also good sources for freelancers. They certainly have marketing needs. BUT--be aware that they might not have a huge budget.
  Who to contact: If it's a really small business, try to connect with the owner.

- **Team up with freelance graphic designers.** You can help each other get work. They might have clients who need copy. And you might have a client who needs design.
  Who to contact: Many graphic designers are on their own when freelancing. So just do an online search for local designers.

- **Advertising agencies** have been a major source of work for me. Even if they have writers on staff, there are times when some agencies have too much work to handle in house and they like to have a pool of dependable freelance copywriters to call on.

Who to contact: In most cases, you want to contact the creative director of an agency. This is typically the person who makes hiring decisions regarding freelancers. You might also want to contact the Human Resources department of larger agencies to ask them how to get on the freelancing list. You should also try to attend advertising events in your area, such as local chapter meetings for the American Advertising Federation, American Marketing Association and Public Relations Society of America.

- **Social media platforms--**like LinkedIn--can be used to find work. But don't just be fishing for jobs on LinkedIn. Instead, join groups and provide value in discussions. Sometimes people will post help wanted posts. I found (and was hired for) a really good gig in the pharmaceutical industry like that.

    Who to contact: Join and contribute to groups in LinkedIn and on Facebook (as well as other social media platforms) that share your interest in writing. Some of the groups I'm in on LinkedIn include: Advertising Copywriting, Advertising Freelance, Content Marketing Institute, LinkEDs & Writers Marketing Communication, Medical Marketing and Communications Group, Public Relations and Communications Professionals, Writers Hangout and Higher Education Marketing & Communications.)

- **Upwork and other job boards** are viable sources for work. Just be careful not to get into a price bidding war that lowers your fees to a point where the work just isn't worth it. Who to contact: There are a lot of job boards out there. Some you can check out include Problogger.com, upwork.com, freelancewritinggigs.com, mediabistro.com, and freelancewriting.com. Get familiar with them and decide which, if any, work for your needs.

- **Former colleagues** are often excellent referral sources. That's why you want to stay in touch with (and stay on good terms with) people you've worked with in the past. Also-- it's just a nice thing to do.

- **Friends and family** can be your informal marketing department. They might know people in their own networks to connect you with. So let people know precisely what you're offering and what you're looking for (industry and projects) so they can sell for you! Tell them what your availability is, too.

How to Connect

Now that you know *who* to connect, the next thing we need to focus on is *how* to connect. Here are some pointers:

- **Cold Calling** Yes, I know. Cold calling can feel yucky--particularly if you've never really done sales before. But it's a viable--and proven--way of getting work. There are TONS of books and resources available that go into the details of how to cold call, but some basic tips I've found helpful are these:

- Talk with the person who makes the decision about hiring freelancers. (Refer to the "who to contact" ideas earlier in this chapter.)
- Know what you're going to say. Write it down if you have to--but don't sound like you're reading it verbatim. A simple cold calling script might look something like this:

"Hi [name of person you're speaking with]! My name is [your name] and I'm a freelance writer who works here in the [city/town] area. The reason I'm calling is to introduce myself and to see if you have a few minutes to discuss your writing needs and how I might be able to help you. Is now a good time?"

If the prospect says "yes"--then ask him or her to share what their writing needs are and then respond with ideas about how you might help.

If the prospect says "no"--ask if there would be a better time to call back. If there is, then make a firm appointment. If the prospect isn't interested, thank them for their time and move on to your next call. No big deal.

- The Law of Averages definitely applies with cold calling. Focus on making a certain number of calls each day rather than obsessing about what the outcome of each call is. Most people aren't going to say "yes" to your services at the time you call. But, if you call enough people, someone is going to need what you're offering.
- Don't feel bad or guilty for cold calling! You're offering a valuable service that businesses need--and you're doing them a favor by letting them know you can help.
- You're going to get more people telling you "no" than saying "yes." And that's perfectly okay. That's the way it works.

Again, it's a numbers game. So don't take "no" personally.

- **Warm Calls/Emails** If a friend, family member, colleague or anyone else makes an introduction with a prospective client for you, this is ideal. In this situation, you can begin your call or email by saying something like this:

"Hi [name of person you're speaking with]! My name is [your name] and I'm a freelance writer who works here in the [city/town] area. [Name of your friend, family member, etc.] mentioned that you might be in need of copywriting services, so I wanted to introduce myself and see if you'd be interested in discussing how I might be able to help you."

- **Attend Events** Networking with other writers, graphic designers, marketing professionals or individuals who are in the industries you want to target (i.e., construction, legal, healthcare, etc.) can really help jumpstart your freelance copywriting career. People like to do business with people they know. And networking events are a great way to make those crucial introductions. Do some research to see which professional groups have local chapters in your area. Also, look for Meetup groups that are of interest to you. Networking might not be the most comfortable thing to do if you're an introvert. But give it a try anyway. It can help you gain traction with your business much faster than just sitting behind a desk.

- **Direct Mail** Don't let any preconceived idea of direct mail turn you off to this marketing tactic. By sending out a simple postcard advertising my services to graphic designers in my local area, I not only landed a very lucrative writing assignment--but I also found an entirely new industry niche that has continued to be a great source of revenue for me.

- **Invite Prospects to Have Coffee (or Lunch, If You Dare)** One of the most effective networking techniques I've used is simply inviting a prospective client out for coffee or lunch. It gives us both a chance to learn more about each other in a setting that's more relaxed than most office or agency environments. Keep it simple. Don't push for work. Give them a chance to talk about what they do and what their needs are. And enjoy yourself! (Also--pick up the tab.)

Chapter 10

10 Commandments of Client Relationships

Establishing a client relationship is only the first step. Building it and maintaining it over time is where the real work--and rewards--come in. How do you do that? Follow the 10 Commandments of Client Relationships. Now, to be clear, they did NOT come down on stone tablets from a mountaintop. But they *are* things I've learned over the years that have helped me build lasting relationships with clients who are good for my business and good for my soul:

1. **Really take the time to get to know your clients business.** Study it. Fall in love with it. Ask for a factory tour. Ask to meet with their

customers. Get to know it better than anyone else--including your client.

2. **Develop a very clear understanding of what your client is looking for**. Ask for a creative brief that includes project objectives, messaging points, must haves, etc. And it needs to be signed off on by client. Also, be sure you fully understand what you're being asked to deliver. If you don't--ASK.

3. **Find out how success of the project will be defined--and by whom.** Will it be defined by a specific person? If so, will you have access to that person? Will be defined by a committee? If so, what's the process for that? In order to achieve success, you need to know what it looks like from your client's perspective.

4. **Be sure to manage a client's expectations from Day 1.** Be clear about what you can do, when you can deliver, how many rounds of changes, your rates, etc. By doing so, everybody knows what to expect from each other—and

that can avoid a lot of frustration in the long run.

5. **Get your fee agreement in writing.** This helps protect both you and your client. They know how much they'll be paying and you know what's expected in return for your fee.

6. **Present your work with confidence--and in person whenever possible.** Don't be apologetic about it. If you don't feel like your copy is great--then don't present it. Only present your best work that provides the best solution. Remember--YOU are the champion of your work. So present it confidently. Doesn't mean client will always love it or that changes won't be needed. But it can go a long way in helping clients have confidence in you and your work.

7. **Don't get defensive when clients ask for changes.** As long as changes are reasonable--make them. If directions are shifted--you might need to renegotiate your fee.

8. **Deliver what you promise when you promise.** No excuses. Don't make your problems your client's problems. Find a way to deliver.

9. **Be easy to work with.** This goes far in terms of getting repeat work. If you're talented, listen well, and are easy to work with—you'll get called back for more work over and over.

10. **Always be providing value.** Help clients think about things in a different way. Do simple things, like sharing articles of interest with them without asking for work. They'll begin to see you not just as someone they're outsourcing work to--but as a valued partner.

Chapter 11
The End. Yet Only the Beginning.

If you've made it this far in the book, CONGRATULATIONS! You're exactly the kind of student I love to coach! Why? Because you're curious about what it takes to become a successful freelance copywriter and you're dedicated to finding out the answers. And that means you're on your way to success before you even get your first client.

One of the main things I've tried to do throughout this book is to provide encouragement and guidance--with a healthy dose of reality. Can you make a really good living as a freelance writer? Yes. Is freelance writing a proven freedom-based business model? Yes. If I had it to do over again, would I make the decision to become a freelance copywriter? Without a doubt. Is it easy to find success? No. It takes work. And commitment. And a willingness to embrace the business aspects of--well--building a business.

Although you've reached the end of this book, you're at the *beginning* of building a rewarding career as a freelance writer. And that's an exciting place to be for a number of reasons, including:

- You'll have the unique opportunity to help others tell the stories of their businesses, their causes, their brands and even themselves in ways that help them connect in a strong and positive way with the audiences they're seeking.

- You'll be providing a HUGE value to your clients by creating clarity and understanding in a very noisy and crowded marketplace.

- You'll always be learning and growing through your exposure to new clients, new industries and new products. And that means you'll stay relevant and needed in a world that's changing faster and faster every year.

- You'll find the FREEDOM you need to build the business and the *life* you want.

I could go on with reason after reason. But I think these make the point pretty well. Now it's just a matter of you making the decision to move forward with your dream of making a living with your writing. I know how scary this can be. But the only way to make the changes you want to make in your life is to do something different. Sometimes that isn't the most comfortable thing in the world. But it can be the most rewarding.

The road to success as a freelance writer--or any type of entrepreneur-- can be a long one. But, if you ask me, it's worth it. SO worth it. I know that *you* have what it takes to make a difference, to create content and experiences that matter, and to build the life you want. So stop reading and get started by applying the principles you've learned in this book! This is *your* time. Now go make the most of it.

Resources

Your FREE *Copy of* **The Prosperous Copywriter's Toolbox**

Want a FREE copy of a comprehensive resource that includes the tools I've used to build a successful freelance copywriting business? It's yours! Go to https://pageturnermission.leadpages.co/prosperouscopywritertoolkit-book1/.

The Page-Turner Mission Freelance Writer Coaching Program

Need some help getting up and going with your new freelance copywriting business?

Have some questions about business or writing--but are having a tough time finding answers?

Looking for a little no-nonsense guidance that will help you get up and going faster?

A "yes' to any of these makes you a great candidate for *The Page-Turner Mission Freelance Writer Coaching Program.* Check out the details at www.pageturnermission/courses. Or email me at mlashley@pageturnermission.com to schedule a time to talk.

Books and Courses and All Kinds of Good Stuff

There are some really great books and courses available to help you hone your skills as a freelance copywriter. Check out some of my favorites www.pageturnermission.com/resources.

The PageTurnerMission.com

Want to learn how to earn with your writing skills? Join us over at www.pageturnermission.com, where your **WRITING SKILLS** and your dream of **MAKING A GREAT LIVING** with them live happily ever after! And become part of our community of writers and entrepreneurs on Facebook (www.facebook.com/pageturnermission) and Twitter (@mlashley)!

About the Author
K.M. Lashley

K.M. Lashley is a freelance copywriter, teacher and entrepreneur living, working and playing in Cary, North Carolina. She's on a mission to help anyone who loves to write find ways to make a great living with their words. And she knows it's possible because she's been doing it for more than 20 years. Join her over at www.pageturnermission.com and on Facebook and Twitter.

Printed in Great Britain
by Amazon